Mesmerizing Poetry - Samuel Moses Veldanda

Samuel Veldanda

Mesmerizing Poetry - Samuel Moses Veldanda
© 2023 Samuel Veldanda

All rights reserved.

No part of this publication may be reproduced,
stored in a retrieval system, or transmitted, in
any form or by any means, electronic,
mechanical, photocopying, recording, or
otherwise, without the prior written permission
of the presenters.

Samuel Veldanda asserts the moral right to be
identified as the author of this work.

Presentation by *BookLeaf Publishing*

Web: www.bookleafpub.com

E-mail: info@bookleafpub.com

ISBN: 9789357744577

First edition 2023

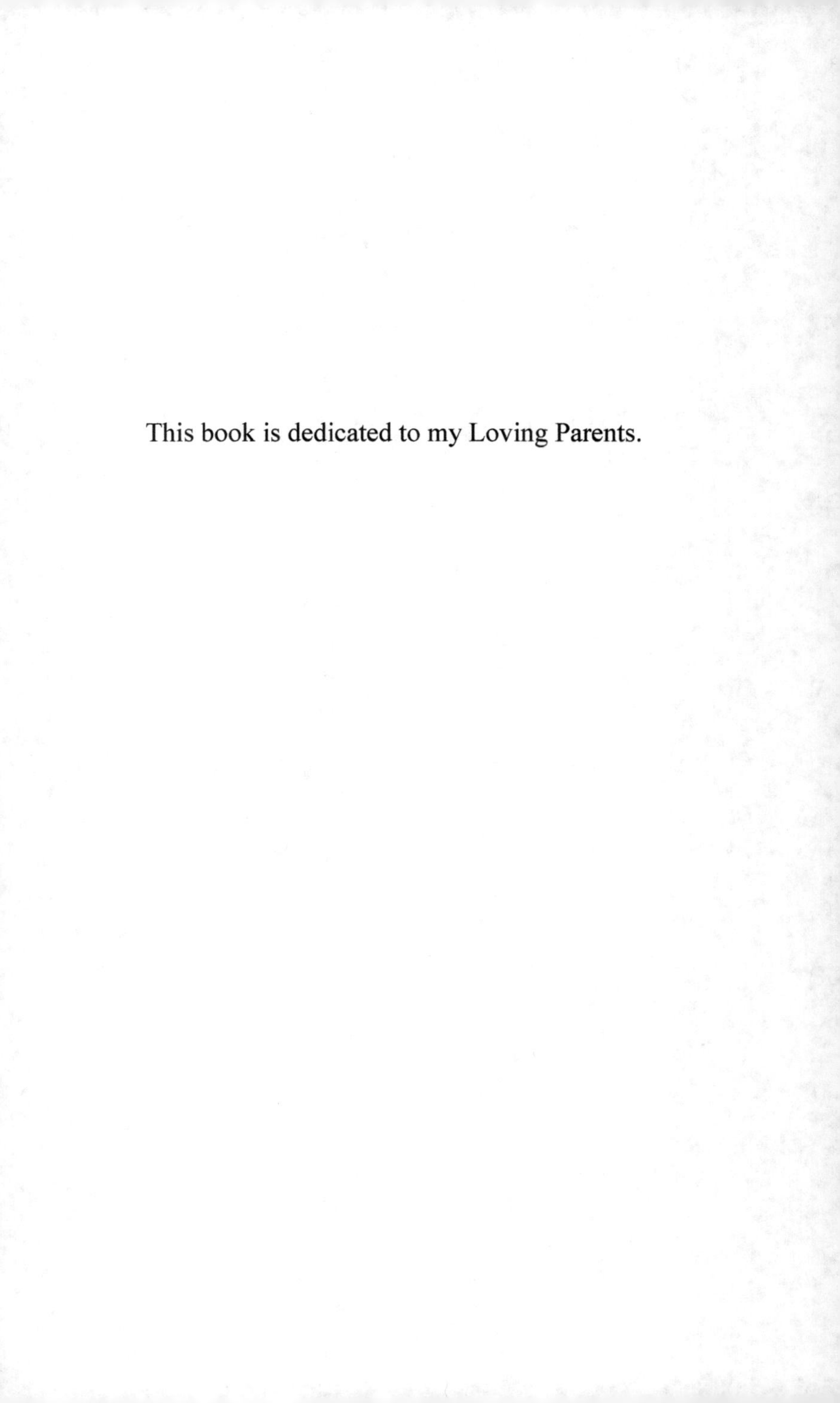

This book is dedicated to my Loving Parents.

ACKNOWLEDGEMENT

"Being grateful is what makes us more humble".

I acknowledge my sincere gratitude to Almighty God because of whom I am who I am. God blessed me with this talent so I'm a poet. The greatest thanksgiving follows to my earthly gods "My parents" because they brought me into this world. My Parents have always supported, helped and facilitated their level best to push me up. Their love is always immense for me so they always allowed me to pursue my own dreams. Not to forget my elder brother Joshua who always appreciates, compliments and pushes me hard to reach many milestones in life. I'm also thankful to my school English teacher Catherine ma'am who showed me how to write poems, who always encouraged and inspired me to write more poems every time. She always helped me no matter what and she even taught me basic poetic devices. Sincere thanks to my graduation English lecturer Padmarao ma'am. She helped me to improve my phonetics, grammar and linguistic skills. She arranged many competitions at the college level, so I was able to participate in all of them, and so I discovered more of my potential in poetry. Thanks to one and all mentioned above, the dearest people for their time, guidance and support.

PREFACE

Samuel, that's me, the original composer/ poet/ author of this masterpiece which is in your hands. I've been a poet since my schooling days. It all started when I was given a topic by my English teacher to compose a poem. It actually took off in an amazing way which really inspired me to create many more pieces. Each poem you read is a part of my life divided and systematically arranged as a volume. All my compositions in the form of poems are present in this book. School, college, and home were the three particular places where I had written as always and the most convenient place I felt to write a poem was "Home sweet home". I write poems when I get a topic, when I get inspiration, as a hobby and most of all whenever I'm elated. You can summarize I just compose poems as I love to that's all I can think of. It was just a hobby and this was an American dream that my poems should be showcased and displayed in libraries so here I get an opportunity to finally bring my pretty dream into reality. You'll definitely be in a mesmerized, majestic, mystical realm when you read my poems.

INDEX

" THE MIRACLE MAKER "

He is the one who has created us
He is the one who has made us

He blesses the blind with eyes
He kindles the humble with a surprise

The one who raises the humble
The one who strengthens the stumble

His eyes are upon the righteous
His teachings are within the fictious

He satisfies those who are in need
He performs the acts according to their deeds

He shows mercy on his people
He strengthens and heals the cripple

He loves his children a lot
For they are not forgot

He saves us from the slay of the evil
He flocks his feather from the devil

He fills us prosperously
He helps us to live eternally

He fills us with his joy
And fills the heart of each boy

He wipes away the tears
He scatters away all the fears

He is our shepherd
Who guides us among the herd

His creation is very beautiful
He does marvels, which are wonderful

He quenches the thirst
He is the first

We adore 'His' beauty
We worship him as a deity

He is our eternal father
And checks what's the matter

He is no one else but God
And saves us by the mighty rod

G - Glorious
O- Over
D - Domains of the Earth

" He " signifies the Supreme one, our heavenly
eternal, loving father.

" MOTHER "

" Just take a glimpse of someone who loves you so
much "

In the life of my dream
You are as soft as cream

Fulfilling all of our destiny,
with a spectacular instancy

Messed up with all burdens
And just speaks about blossoming gardens

Hiding off every trouble
By making it a fable

Just desires that we should learn
And learn to earn

(This is the person who enlightens your life with
tremendous joy that is unending and also satisfies
your needs. Whom we call as.... MOTHER, MOM,
MUMMA, MAA, MUMMY, MUM)

" SISTER "

I have a precious gemstone
Of a perfect tone

It's a jewel in my heart
That can never be apart

It's more costly than diamond
Essential than almond

You can't rate her beauty
You can't call her sweety

She's sweeter than sugar
Don't mess with my sugar

She knows all my secrets
She knows all my favourites

She's as cold as ice
She's as hot as spice

She works for her passion
She styles up for fashion

She's her father's lovebird
She's her mother's thick curd

She loves me like a mother
For she's none other

Don't you know, mister
You see, she's my sister

" TEACHER "

I am the person loved by all
Children and parents frequently call

Knowledge, discipline, and improvement are in my
dictionary
Wisdom, love, and service are in my visionary

Many times I've been judged
To display my skills and talents, I've been urged

Literacy and perfection are my obligations
Sincerity and punctuality are my regulations

Hardwork and dedication are needed the most
Proving myself that I'm fit for the post

I take care and I love you
I feed you and I help you

Looking at you I remember my past
Not forgetting my memories are vast

I can be right, I can be wrong
Not always I can sing my own song

I look after you as a parent
It's my duty that I've been sent

I'm God's glorious, beautiful creature
You all know me as I'm your teacher

" STRUCTOSTEM "
(Structure of Language, Story of Writing, Education System)

A to Z forms the letters
Making our life sensible and better

Letters were less as the world is large
Words came up and became in charge

Words don't matter much
The phrases spoke the truth, such

Phrasal appraisal didn't last longer
As sentences arose and stayed stronger

Old were the sentences
Paragraphs were the next intense

Paragraphs were worn out
Passages became more stout

Passages were traced on palm leaves
As these were the ancient sleeves

Manuscripts were eaten by insects
Inscriptions sprang up as new context

Don't use leaf and not a metal
For writing purpose use Papyrus petal

Lately papyrus lost its glory
Paper in turn created new story

Tell the stories to a child
And fiction for the grown up wild

Kindergarten is for tiny toads
School as Temple is for extreme explodes

Pre and post- schooling done
College and university will be the next one

Smarty,naughty,plumpy kiddos in primary grades
Young spirited, fierce lads in secondary grades

Independent, cool,mature teens in tertiary grades
This is how the Education System parades.

" TIME "

Time is so precious
It's very felicitous
Time has got no end
You have to change your trend

Don't be too late
Never blame your fate
Always be quick on time
Just as a quick lime

Early bird catches worm
So you have to be very firm
Time and tide waits for none
Therefore be the first one

We are very lazy
We become very dizzy
Time's ahead is hard to see
Time's begone we fail to be

Every second, every minute
Be on time within the limit
Every hour, every day
Look to the clock while on the way

Seasons may change days may pass by
But time repeats aloud Oh! my my
Save your time before the gloom
Or else it will be the day of doom

" BLAZING SUMMER "

Right on a sunny morning
Right on a sunny day
Peeped at my little window
Up out today

Right on a sunny morning
Right on a sunny day
Feeling lucky and happy
To rise up after a nappy

Look here and there
Look out everywhere
Look for sun is shining
Over the day glancing

Winter has gone
And summer has come
Now autumn has left
Look spring has arrived

The brisky blaze of sun
The bright face of sun
Spreading out everywhere
Blooming with the radiance

Right on a sunny morning
Right on a sunny day
The breeze is blowing
And the winds go flowing

The sunflowers arising
The daffodils go rising
Roses get to know
That sun has arose

Sweet smelling meadows
Clear green plain fields
Beasts of the forests
Birds of the sky

Creatures of the under water
Creatures of the ocean
Trees & plants & herbs & shrubs
All depend on the sun

Look out there's a sun shining
Look out there's a rainbow
Look out for the oceans
That flow and glow and row

Right on a sunny morning
Right on a sunny day
Look out there's a sun smiling
And blushing back to me

" FLOWERS "

Flowers are beautiful
Flowers are colourful
Flowers are brightful
Flowers are plentiful

Flowers are in shape
Flowers are in size
Flowers are in colour
Flowers are in type

Flowers are precious
Flowers are marvellous
Flowers are bright
Flowers are upright

Flowers give fragrance
Flowers spread magnificence
Flowers rarely gloom
Flowers constantly bloom

Flowers are loved by all
Flowers are big and small
Flowers are means for appreciation
Flowers are God's glorious creation

"MASSACRE OF FEMALE FOETUS "

When a child is born
We blow the horn

Boy or girl? that's the big question
After carrying out the huge operation

Sex determination is the first priority
Pregnancy arrives, and it's a great difficulty

Knowing it's a boy, let him live
It's his birthright, let him survive

Get to know it's a girl, kill her now
Don't give her a chance, to make us bow

Village or city, the situation is the same
Girl child always carries the blame

For a man you need a wife
When she conceives a girl, you seize her life

Gender discrimination is the main basis
Carried out as an old traditional crisis

Girl child is aborted, it's a big luxury
Freed from responsibility and from dowry

Girl child is detected
Female foeticide is subjected

Female foeticide is a malpractice
Give it a pause and follow new tactics

Abort her, get rid of her
Murder her, as we don't need her

Boys are a blessing, girls are a disgrace
She can't stand strong, she'll lose the race

Don't cut our noses and bring us shame
By giving birth to girls and disowning our name

Girls are a burden, boys are a boon
Kick the womb and kill her soon

Sex determination : say no more
For precious girl child open up the door

Formulation of laws and abiding by it
To save girl child and making it lit

Keeping a watch on village and city
Ensuring female foeticide is banned so pretty

Take legal action against these scoundrels
File up strict cases against such criminals

Spreading social awareness is our responsibility
To achieve gender equality, let's use all our ability

Life without a girl child is a big hell
Blame's on you so you'll be in prison cell

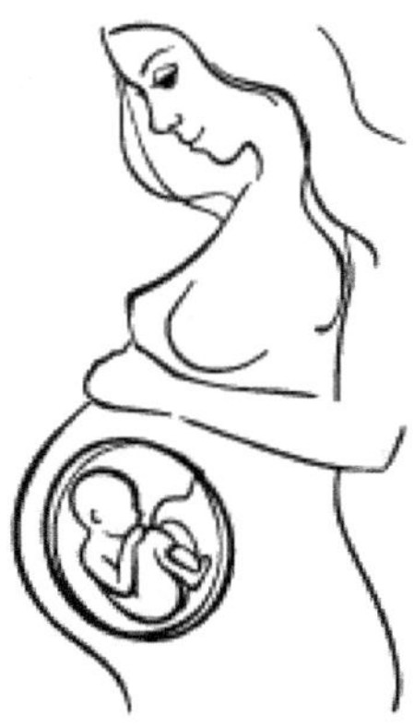

" WOMAN "

In country, town or city
There's always a female so pretty

Though found in different ages
Big or small all around in various stages

Bursting of curses in her infancy
Blaming a girl for her delicacy

Poking, picking and eve-teasing at her teens
Touching, harassing and staring at every moment so
keen

Making her conceive and let her alone
Exploit her, torment her, and make her mourn

Demand her dowry for marriage
Kick her out as unwanted luggage

Making her a mother and asking her to care
Loading all responsibilities, which is not so fair

Cooking, cleaning, caring for all
Hungry, unclean , not cared by all

Keeping restrictions during her periods
Gender discrimination in open myriads

Infant girl, teenage girl, whoever they may be
Adult women, old women are always on their knee

Daughter, sister, wife, and mother
Roles of women played by one another

A woman to recall
Is God's greatest gift of all

W - Working, wonderful women
O - Outstanding, optimistic girls
M - Marvellous ,magnanimous mothers
A - Amazing, aspiring all rounders
N - Noble, nice ladies.

" TSUNAMI "

A large big wave
When people go into cave

Many were brave
Some did save

The waves were high
People did cry

In time of need
People did feed

Everyone were scared
But they cared

Let's face the fear
And be of good cheer

" CREATION "

Creation's story is a big mystery
As scientists have their own history

Creation is far more than imagination
Let's look for it's navigation

The heavens, the earth, the light
The sun & moon & stars so bright

Light and darkness were separated
Day and night were all created

The firmament wanted lights above
To show signs, seasons, years, and days all below

Fishes took birth in the seas and oceans
Birds took flight in bright azure sky

Insects in burrows, animals on lands
They live in forests and on grasslands

Grasses and herbs, shrubs and bushes
Creepers, climbers and trees in line rushes

Fields and plains, plateaus and mountains
Meadows and hills, brooks and fountains

Creation's story is no longer mystery
And it has got it's way big history

Spontaneous theory, big bang theory
Has no meaning and becomes weary

All theories have got no other history
For God's Creation was the biggest mystery

Creator always hid Himself
In the Paradise by Himself

For He has made this all
The Earth big round like ball

So all the glory, all the thanks, and
All the blessings to His matchless name.

(Inspired by Creation's History from The Holy Bible
- Genesis Chapter 1)

" UPS & DOWNS IN ENVIRONMENT "

The land before time was filled with originality
As time lapsed, land lost all its formality

Ages evolved, and nature transformed
Humanity arose, and the biosphere deformed

Development paved a way, technology had to stay
Flora & fauna were forced to pay, so nature's left with
no ray

Global warming, disasters, and pollution took the
lead
Extinction, poaching, and loss of habitat were the
next indeed

Time flows by and the tables turn
Pandemic originates and is the next intern

Deaths, disasters, destruction strikes off humanity
COVID encroaches and encounters the whole
popularity

Environmental grounds become reckless and care -
free
As Lockdown's effect turns out, biomes are set - free

Coronavirus enters, so ecosystems restore
Plants, fishes, birds, and animals behave like before

Humanity's absence made a huge difference
Environmental healing displayed it's occurrence

Man felt like caged and prisoned
Lockdown's benefit animals were secluded and freed

Urban and rural life became abnormal
Wildlife rather freed from dangers acted normal

Mortal deaths ranked up so high
Trees again started to cry

Usage of sanitizers, disinfectants and masks becomes
a waste
Soil takes up all these non eco-friendly in such a
haste

Lockdown's resultant effect is improved quality of air
Ecologically speaking balance is maintained which is
so fair

Pandemic breaks in and brings these many changes
As we can see nature's restoration, rehabilitation and
rejuvenation with wide ranges.

" BROTHER "

Brothers are of different race
They add up flavour and more grace

The strongest support system and backbone
You can't compare him with no one

Boys will be boys and brothers are like no other
Mischief filled naughty lads which mostly bothers

Mostly sweet and sometimes spicy
Without their existence life remains icy

They do work which stays invisible
As all suspect them just to scribble and dribble

Brothers do fight which they have to do
If they won't do it's strange for you

Younger brother or elder brother
Remains always a pet of mother

Behaving like a father is his habit
Instincts do matter which make him inhabit

Brother's love is abundantly immense
Which remains forever and is so deep and intense

" FAMILY "

Life is full of love
Which comes down from above

Love is deeply rooted
Its existence can never be looted

You may loot a person's treasure
You fail to shoot a person's precious pleasure

The greatest treasure
Which has no unit to measure

Its measurements are higher than the sky
Deeper than the ocean and can never go dry

Seasons may go dry or wet
But some things in Life you can never bet

It's so mysterious to bet on and rare to compare
It's got no end and something you can't share

Let me share a secret for your curiosity
Expecting in return good relations and generosity

Accepting your generosity let me tell you happily
For I was discussing about " My Family "

" FATHER "

You may find me strict
As you can never predict

I may be hard
For I have to always guard

I formulate rule and regulations
I make conditions and obligations

I do rule and be the head
I admit you to school and carry you to bed

You will rarely call
For you may not recall

You may not feel it and won't discuss with one
another
Open up your eyes and see behind it's me your father

" STUDENT "

It's hard being a student, as most of us say
Well, I'm one of them let's watch what to play

Being a teacher's pet does not always suits me I bet
Wanting to be one, can't say I'm not fit to be that one
yet

I go by different names
For I've performed many acts and gained fame

Who understands my struggles and my feelings
Well none other than a student who can do the
healing

With many expectations, I'm born to fulfill
Not knowing one of them, I just try to chill

Being a child or a teen doesn't matter
Being a student you ought to chatter

Carrying responsibilities isn't my cup of tea
Taking so much pressure upon me I totally disagree

Living life to the fullest is my American dream
Just don't know yet who'll add that flavour to my
cream

During class lectures I'm in my dreamland
Not knowing when I'll be back to my wonderland

Daydreaming and nap taking is my duty
Aiming to fulfill it I do with beauty

A lot many times people become judgmental
Not realizing I'm very open and gentle

Partial treatments are my day's routine
Can't figure out why people are so mean

Discipline and great behaviour is expected at all
times
But being one , in return I receive no appraisal
rhymes

I'm good at heart if you could only see
I'm not a criminal which you assumed I would be

I'm a normal person like you
Believe me or not I'm honest and true

Would you like to be my friend ?
Hey I'm a student on whom you can always depend

" WATER "

Life's precious, pure possession
Found in different forms is my confession

Glaciers and snow make one of its state
Vapours of light-weight are next to relate

Lakes, ponds, rivers and streams
Brooks, waterfalls they all gleam

Rain or marine both matter a lot
Seas and Oceans cover the whole plot

' The Universal solvent ' is my tagline
Life giving resource is costlier than wine

The home for all aquatic beings
You disturb it, it may hurt their feelings

Saline or fresh water both are useful
Hot or cold water both are fruitful

Wasting and polluting it may cost our lives
Cause without water we may not survive

The concluding talk says it all
Water's hidden story is not so small

" LOVE "

Love is blind as most folks say
Love has many forms which rarely display

The most purest, abundant and selfless form
'Agape Love' being the first to perform

God's love is so divine
Unconditional love which never declines

' Storge ' being the second which binds the fam
Connects parents and children making them adhesive
like jam

It's the most natural of loves
More original than twitter-pating doves

Third being ' Philia ' the most friendly
Love between friends and equals which happens
accidentally

Love of friends has got no end
Truest form of all will never bend

'Eros' the most renowned in them
Passionate Love is an erotic gem

It's between couples who love with passion
Sometimes it goes out of control and becomes an
obsession

So love can strike like a lightning storm
Or fade away quickly because of a standard norm

Love has got no boundaries
Love doesn't think of unnecessary worries

Love can't be measured by any instrument
Love has got no rules which ain't implement

Friends or enemies, love them all
Kith and kin or strangers will be loved as I recall

So this is love so mystical, mysterious and majestic
As it has no heights, hindrances and is holistic

" WHO AM I ? "

Who am I , the glorious one or gloomy soul ?
I know that I'm a fearfully and wonderfully created
soul

Who am I, the good lad or the bad guy?
Well I'm mostly good but don't ask why

Who am I very young or too old ?
You see I'm fierce & enthusiastic young alongside I'm
wise and the purest gold

Who am I, the righteous or the sinner ?
Now that's something you need to ask when I'm the
ultimate winner

Who am I, creative or destructive ?
It totally depends upon the situation but mostly I
prefer to be productive

Who am I the introvert or an extrovert ?
Can't say I'm a mixture of both why to take the extra
effort

Who am I, blessed or cursed ?
All I can say is I'm blessed beyond measure so yes
I'm always blessed

Who am I lover or a hater ?
I'm loved by all and so they make me greater

Who am I pretty handsome or shabby ugly ?
I know this , that I'm good looking so yes I'm lovely

Who am I after all?
It's none other than the poet himself that's the
incredible master of all .